# O'Leary

## by Iain Gray

GW00643417

Lang**Syne**

PUBLISHING

WRITING *to* REMEMBER

**LangSyne**

**PUBLISHING**

WRITING *to* REMEMBER

79 Main Street, Newtongrange,
Midlothian EH22 4NA
Tel: 0131 344 0414   Fax: 0845 075 6085
E-mail: info@lang-syne.co.uk
www.langsyneshop.co.uk

Design by Dorothy Meikle
Printed by Printwell Ltd
© Lang Syne Publishers Ltd 2016

ISBN 978-1-85217-410-1

# O'Leary

**MOTTO:**
Strong is the king of the sea
(or) Strong on land and on the sea.

**CREST:**
An arm in armour, holding a sword.

**NAME** variations include:
Lary
Laury
Learey
Learie
Leary
O'Leery
O'Laoghaire *(Gaelic)*
O'Laoire *(Gaelic)*
O'Laohaire *(Gaelic)*
Uí Laoghaire *(Gaelic)*

*Chapter one:*

# Origins of Irish surnames

**According to an old saying, there are two types of Irish – those who actually are Irish and those who wish they were.**

This sentiment is only one example of the allure that the high romance and drama of the proud nation's history holds for thousands of people scattered across the world today.

It's a sad fact, however, that the vast majority of Irish surnames are found far beyond Irish shores, rather than on the Emerald Isle itself.

The population stood at around eight million souls in 1841, but today it stands at fewer than six million.

This is mainly a tragic consequence of the potato famine, also known as the Great Hunger, which devastated Ireland between 1845 and 1849.

The Irish peasantry had become almost wholly reliant for basic sustenance on the potato, first introduced from the Americas in the seventeenth century.

When the crop was hit by a blight, at least 800,000 people starved to death while an estimated two million others were forced to seek a new life far from their native shores – particularly in America, Canada, and Australia.

The effects of the potato blight continued until about 1851, by which time a firm pattern of emigration had become established.

Ireland's loss, however, was to the gain of the countries in which the immigrants settled, contributing enormously, as their descendants do today, to the well being of the nations in which their forefathers settled.

But those who were forced through dire circumstance to establish a new life in foreign parts never forgot their roots, or the proud heritage and traditions of the land that gave them birth.

Nor do their descendants.

It is a heritage that is inextricably bound up in the colourful variety of Irish names themselves – and the origin and history of these names forms an integral part of the vibrant drama that is the nation's history, one of both glorious fortune and tragic misfortune.

This history is well documented, and one of the most important and fascinating of the earliest sources are *The Annals of the Four Masters*, compiled between 1632 and 1636 by four friars at the Franciscan Monastery in County Donegal.

Compiled from earlier sources, and purporting to go back to the Biblical Deluge, much of the material takes in the mythological origins and history of Ireland and the Irish.

This includes tales of successive waves of invaders and settlers such as the Fomorians, the Partholonians, the Nemedians, the Fir Bolgs, the Tuatha De Danann, and the Laigain.

Of particular interest are the *Milesian Genealogies*,

because the majority of Irish clans today claim a descent from either Heremon, Ir, or Heber – three of the sons of Milesius, a king of what is now modern day Spain.

These sons invaded Ireland in the second millennium B.C, apparently in fulfilment of a mysterious prophecy received by their father.

This Milesian lineage is said to have ruled Ireland for nearly 3,000 years, until the island came under the sway of England's King Henry II in 1171 following what is known as the Cambro-Norman invasion.

This is an important date not only in Irish history in general, but for the effect the invasion subsequently had for Irish surnames.

'Cambro' comes from the Welsh, and 'Cambro-Norman' describes those Welsh knights of Norman origin who invaded Ireland.

But they were invaders who stayed, inter-marrying with the native Irish population and founding their own proud dynasties that bore Cambro-Norman names such as Archer, Barbour, Brannagh, Fitzgerald, Fitzgibbon, Fleming, Joyce, Plunkett, and Walsh – to name only a few.

These 'Cambro-Norman' surnames that still flourish throughout the world today form one of the three main categories in which Irish names can be placed – those of Gaelic-Irish, Cambro-Norman, and Anglo-Irish.

Previous to the Cambro-Norman invasion of the twelfth century, and throughout the earlier invasions and settlement of those wild bands of sea rovers known as the Vikings in the eighth and ninth centuries, the population of the island was relatively small, and it was normal for a person to be identified through the use of only a forename.

But as population gradually increased and there were many more people with the same forename, surnames were adopted to distinguish one person, or one community, from another.

Individuals identified themselves with their own particular tribe, or 'tuath', and this tribe – that also became known as a clann, or clan – took its name from some distinguished ancestor who had founded the clan.

The Gaelic-Irish form of the name Kelly, for example, is Ó Ceallaigh, or O'Kelly, indicating descent from an original 'Ceallaigh', with the 'O' denoting 'grandson of.' The name was later anglicised to Kelly.

The prefix 'Mac' or 'Mc', meanwhile, as with the clans of the Scottish Highlands, denotes 'son of.'

Although the Irish clans had much in common with their Scottish counterparts, one important difference lies in what are known as 'septs', or branches, of the clan.

Septs of Scottish clans were groups who often bore an entirely different name from the clan name but were under the clan's protection.

In Ireland, septs were groups that shared the same name and who could be found scattered throughout the four provinces of Ulster, Leinster, Munster, and Connacht.

The 'golden age' of the Gaelic-Irish clans, infused as their veins were with the blood of Celts, pre-dates the Viking invasions of the eighth and ninth centuries and the Norman invasion of the twelfth century, and the sacred heart of the country was the Hill of Tara, near the River Boyne, in County Meath.

Known in Gaelic as 'Teamhar na Rí', or Hill of Kings, it was the royal seat of the 'Ard Rí Éireann', or High King of Ireland, to whom the petty kings, or chieftains, from the island's provinces were ultimately subordinate.

It was on the Hill of Tara, beside a stone pillar known as the Irish 'Lia Fáil', or Stone of Destiny, that the High Kings were inaugurated and, according to legend, this stone would emit a piercing screech that could be heard all over Ireland when touched by the hand of the rightful king.

The Hill of Tara is today one of the island's main tourist attractions.

Opposition to English rule over Ireland, established in the wake of the Cambro-Norman invasion, broke out frequently and the harsh solution adopted by the powerful forces of the Crown was to forcibly evict the native Irish from their lands.

These lands were then granted to Protestant colonists, or 'planters', from Britain.

Many of these colonists, ironically, came from Scotland and were the descendants of the original 'Scotti', or 'Scots', who gave their name to Scotland after migrating there in the fifth century A.D., from the north of Ireland.

Colonisation entailed harsh penal laws being imposed on the majority of the native Irish population, stripping them practically of all of their rights.

The Crown's main bastion in Ireland was Dublin and its environs, known as the Pale, and it was the dispossessed peasantry who lived outside this Pale, desperately striving to eke out a meagre living.

It was this that gave rise to the modern-day expression of someone or something being 'beyond the pale'.

Attempts were made to stamp out all aspects of the ancient Gaelic-Irish culture, to the extent that even to bear a Gaelic-Irish name was to invite discrimination.

This is why many Gaelic-Irish names were anglicised with, for example, and noted above, Ó Ceallaigh, or O'Kelly, being anglicised to Kelly.

Succeeding centuries have seen strong revivals of Gaelic-Irish consciousness, however, and this has led to many families reverting back to the original form of their name, while the language itself is frequently found on the fluent tongues of an estimated 90,000 to 145,000 of the island's population.

Ireland's turbulent history of religious and political strife is one that lasted well into the twentieth century, a landmark century that saw the partition of the island into the twenty-six counties of the independent Republic of

Ireland, or Eire, and the six counties of Northern Ireland, or Ulster.

Dublin, originally founded by Vikings, is now a vibrant and truly cosmopolitan city while the proud city of Belfast is one of the jewels in the crown of Ulster.

It was Saint Patrick who first brought the light of Christianity to Ireland in the fifth century A.D.

Interpretations of this Christian message have varied over the centuries, often leading to bitter sectarian conflict – but the many intricately sculpted Celtic Crosses found all over the island are symbolic of a unity that crosses the sectarian divide.

It is an image that fuses the 'old gods' of the Celts with Christianity.

All the signs from the early years of this new millennium indicate that sectarian strife may soon become a thing of the past – with the Irish and their many kinsfolk across the world, be they Protestant or Catholic, finding common purpose in the rich tapestry of their shared heritage.

*Chapter two:*

# Hereditary lords

**With a rich heritage steeped in Irish myth and legend, the O'Learys are particularly associated with the present day county of Cork, in the ancient province of Munster, where there are two Ballyleary place names.**

It is in Co. Cork that they flourished from earliest times, and where many of the name are to be found to this day.

The main Gaelic form of the name is O'Laoghaire, with 'Laoghaire' formerly a personal name indicating 'herdsman' or 'keeper of the calves' – with 'laogh' the Gaelic for 'calf' and 'aire' meaning 'keeper'.

The historical figure from whom the O'Learys trace their name and descent is the early fifth century High King of Ireland known as Laoghaire.

His fame throughout the Emerald Isle was such that he also gave his name to what today is the bustling harbour and port of Dún Laoghaire ('Fort of Laoghaire'), anglicised as Dunleary, south of Dublin.

One other indication of the ancient pedigree of the O'Learys is that it can be traced back through the dim mists of time to when historical fact becomes entwined with Celtic myth and legend.

Along with other proud native Irish clans that include the O'Donovans and the O'Keefes, their name is associated with the mythical Clíodhna, a Queen of the Banshees identified with the early settlers to the Emerald Isle known as the Tuatha De Danann.

It is in the area of the original O'Leary territory of Rosscarbery, in Co. Cork, that her wails can still be heard, portending ill fortune for those who hear her.

But this is only one aspect of Clíodhna who, according to some legends, is a goddess of beauty and love who left the otherworldly land of promise, Tairngire, to join her mortal lover Ciabhán.

As Ciabhán left her sleeping on the shore near present day Glandore harbour to engage in a hunt, she was swept by a wave back to Tairngire, never to return and never to be reunited with her lover.

The tide at Glandore harbour, where Clíodhna is said to sleep, is known to this day as Tonn Clíodhna – Clíodhna's Wave.

Hereditary lords of Rosscarbery, the O'Learys, part of the Corca Laidhe tribal grouping, were also hereditary wardens of the famed seat of higher learning known as the School of Ross.

Founded near Rosscarbery in the sixth century by St Fachtna, whose feast day is August 14, it was renowned for centuries, attracting scholars not only from Ireland itself but also from much further afield.

In the wake of the late twelfth century Norman invasion of the island and the subsequent consolidation of the power of the English Crown, the O'Learys, in common with other native Irish clans, found themselves pushed from their original territory to make way for Anglo-Norman adventurers and settlers.

The O'Learys managed to remain in Co. Cork, but were pushed north-eastwards to the region of Uibh Laoghaire, or Inchigeelagh, where they held sway as chiefs under the overall rule of their powerful allies, the MacCarthys of Muskerry.

Rebellions against the power of the Crown were frequent and bloody, mainly fuelled by the English Crown's policy of settling, or 'planting' loyal Protestants on land held by English Catholics.

This policy had started during the reign from 1491 to 1547 of Henry VIII, whose Reformation effectively outlawed the established Roman Catholic faith throughout his dominions.

Rebellion erupted against the increasingly harsh treatment of the native Irish in 1594, under the command of Hugh O'Neill, 2nd Earl of Tyrone, and the O'Donnell chieftain Red Hugh O'Donnell – with the O'Leary chief Auliffe O'Leary and his kinsman Mahon O'Leary fighting in the ranks of the O'Neills.

In what is known as *Cogadh na Naoi mBliama*, or the Nine Years War, the rebels engaged in a vicious campaign of guerrilla warfare, inflicting a number of significant defeats on the forces of the Crown.

As English control over Ireland hung precariously in the

balance, thousands of more troops, including mercenaries, were hastily despatched to the island and, in the face of the overwhelming odds against them, O'Neill and O'Donnell sought help from Spain.

A Spanish army under General del Aquila landed at Kinsale in December of 1601, but was forced into surrender only a few weeks later, in January of 1602.

Resistance continued until 1603, but proved abortive, and as punishment for their active role in the rebellion, it was ordered that the O'Learys – in common with other rebels – should have their lands confiscated.

They managed to retain most of them, however, because what had become their main territory of the mountainous region of Inchigeelagh was virtually inaccessible to all but the most determined land-grabber.

But all this changed in the wake of the devastating Cromwellian invasion and conquest of 1649.

England's 'Lord Protector' descended on Ireland at the head of a 20,000-strong army that landed at Ringford, and an early warning of the terrors that were in store for the native Catholic Irish came when Drogheda was stormed and between 2,000 and 4,000 of its inhabitants killed.

The defenders of the town's St. Peter's Church were burned to death as they huddled for refuge in the steeple and the church deliberately torched, while a similar fate awaited Wexford, on the southeast coast, where at least 1,500 of its inhabitants were slaughtered.

Cromwell's troopers were given free rein to hunt down and kill priests, while rebel estates were confiscated, including those of the O'Learys.

In return, they were given pathetically small estates west of the river Shannon – where they were hemmed in by colonies of Cromwellian troopers and their families.

The final collapse of the ancient Gaelic Order of clans came in the aftermath of what is known in Ireland as *Cogadh an Dá Rí*, or The War of the Two Kings.

This was ignited in 1688 when the Stuart monarch James II was deposed and fled into exile in France and was replaced on the throne by William of Orange and his wife Mary.

The war ended in Ireland only after much bloodshed between the supporters of the two kings, and the signing of the Treaty of Limerick in September of 1691 – under the terms of which those who were willing to swear an oath of loyalty to William were allowed to remain in their native land.

Those not willing to do so, including many native Irish such as the O'Learys, reluctantly chose exile.

*Chapter three:*

# A literary tradition

**A series of harsh measures known as the Penal Laws were put into effect following the 1691 Treaty of Limerick.**

Under their terms Catholics were barred from the legal profession, the armed forces and parliament and not allowed to bear arms or own a horse worth more than £5.

All Roman Catholic clergy and bishops were officially 'banished' from the island in 1697, while it has been estimated that by 1703 less than 15% of the land was owned by Irish Catholics.

Art O'Leary, known in his native language as Airt Uí Laoghaire, and who also became the subject of what today is still considered one of the greatest laments and love poems ever written, was one of the many victims of the harsh Penal Laws.

One of the few remaining members of the hard-pressed Roman Catholic gentry and barred from a worthwhile career in his native land, he was educated on the Continent and later rose through the ranks of Empress Marie Theresa's Army of Austro-Hungary to serve as a captain in the Hungarian Hussars.

His family home in Ireland was Rathleigh House, near Macroom, in the O'Leary heartland of Co. Cork, and it was to here that he returned from the Continent and, in 1767, married the widowed Irish noblewoman Eileen O'Connell.

He fell foul of the Penal Laws in 1773 when he refused to sell his fine white horse to Abraham Morris, the Protestant Sheriff of Cork, for the paltry and derisory sum of £5 that the sheriff 'offered'.

Morris had long coveted the horse whose forehead, according to the subsequent lament, "bore a snow-white star", and abused his authority to have O'Leary declared an outlaw and a price of twenty guineas put on his head.

O'Leary went on the run, but was ambushed by Morris and a party of soldiers at Carraig an Ime and brutally shot dead.

His horse is said to have raced back to Rathleigh House covered in blood, and Art's faithful wife, although heavily pregnant at the time with her sixth child, mounted the steed and galloped back to Carraig an Ime where she found her husband's body.

So great was her grief that she wrote the lament to her dead husband known as *Caoineadh Airt Uí Laoghaire - Lament for Art O'Leary*.

Describing Art's life and death and calling for revenge on his murderers, the 390-line epic poem has also been described as "the most remarkable set of keening verses to have survived."

A few weeks after O'Leary's murder, his brother Cornelius attempted to murder Morris in revenge – but the sheriff survived his gun shot wounds and O'Leary fled to America.

Later submitting himself to trial, so great was the public outcry over Art O'Leary's murder, Morris was nevertheless found 'innocent of any crime' – but he died shortly afterwards as a result of the wounds inflicted earlier by O'Leary's brother.

In keeping with the great Irish literary tradition of which Art O'Leary's widow Eileen became a shining light through *Caoineadh Airt Uí Laoghaire*, Father Peadar O'Laoghaire, known to English readers as Father Peter O'Leary, was the Roman Catholic priest and writer born in 1839 in Clondrchid parish, Co. Cork.

Recognised as one of the founders of modern Irish literature, he was ordained a priest in 1867 and served in a number of parishes until settling at Castlelyons in 1891 – and it was from here that he penned some of his greatest works.

Most noted of these is *Séadna*, first published in 1904 through serialisation in Irish language newspapers.

His autobiography, *Mo Sgéal Féin – My Own Life* – was published before his death in 1920.

Back to the field of battle, another bearer of the O'Leary name who gained distinction beyond Ireland's shores was Daniel O'Leary, who was born in Cork in 1802.

The son of a butter merchant, he rose to become a Brigadier General in the army of the South American revolutionary Simón Bolivar, known as the Liberator, who led independence movements against Spanish rule.

O'Leary died in Bogotá, Columbia, in 1854.

One O'Leary who certainly pursued a varied and distinguished career was Michael O'Leary, a First World War Irish recipient of the Victoria Cross, the highest award for bravery in the face of enemy action for British and Commonwealth forces.

Born in 1890 in Inchigeelagh, Co. Cork, he had served in the Royal Navy, followed by the Irish Guards, before immigrating to Canada in 1913 to serve in Saskatchewan with the Royal North-West Mounted Police.

He returned to Europe shortly after the outbreak of war in 1914 to enlist in the British Army – and it was as a lance-corporal with his old regiment, the Irish Guards, that he was awarded the Victoria Cross after charging and destroying two heavily defended German barricades near the French village of Cuinchy.

Following his brave actions, he was featured for a time on army recruitment posters.

He returned to Canada with his family in 1921 to serve with the Ontario Provincial Police – before returning to Britain yet again on the outbreak of the Second World War in 1939.

He served as a captain in the Middlesex regiment before being put in command of prisoner of war camps in the south of England; he died in 1961.

Back to Ireland and the O'Leary's great literary tradition, John O'Leary was the celebrated poet and nationalist who was born in 1830 in Tipperary.

A member of the Irish Republican Brotherhood and editor of the nationalist *The Irish People*, he served nine years of a 20-year prison sentence for his republican activities before going into exile in Paris in 1874.

Returning to Ireland eleven years later along with his sister, the poet Ellen O'Leary, he became a prominent literary figure along with friends and contemporaries who included W.B. Yeats, Rose Kavanagh, Katharine Tynan and Maude Gonne.

His death in 1907 was lamented a number of years later by Yeats in his poem September 1913, with the memorable line:

> *Romantic Ireland's dead and gone;*
> *it's with O'Leary in the grave.*

Two other bearers of the name of John O'Leary have also been involved in Irish politics.

Born in 1933 in Dunrine, Killarney, John O'Leary is the former Irish Fianna Fáil politician who served from 1966 to 1997 as TD (member in the Irish Parliament known as the Dáil) for Kerry South.

The other John O'Leary, who was born in 1894 and died in 1959, was the Irish Labour Party politician who was first elected to the Dáil in 1943, as the TD for Wexford.

O'Learys have also gained distinction in the justiciary –

notably Sir Humphrey O'Leary, born in 1886 in Blenheim, New Zealand, who served as Chief Justice of New Zealand from 1946 until his death in 1953.

Bearers of the O'Leary name have also gained distinction at an international level through a diverse range of other skills and pursuits.

*Chapter four:*

# On the world stage

**Born to Irish parents in 1973 in Colchester, England, Dermot O'Leary is the radio and television presenter whose broadcasting career began as a disc jockey with Radio Essex.**

Host of his own show on BBC Radio 2, he has also been the presenter of the popular British television talent show *The X-Factor* since 2007.

With film credits that include the 2000 *Mom's Got a Date with a Vampire* and the 2009 *Sorority Row*, **Matt O'Leary** is the American actor who was born in 1987 in Chicago.

His television credits include *CSI: Crime Scene Investigation* and *Law and Order: Criminal Intent*, while also in America **Denis Leary** is the comedian, actor, director and writer who was born in 1957 in Worcester, Massachusetts.

The son of Irish immigrants, at the time of writing he is also the co-creator and star of the American television show *Rescue Me*, for which he received a 2005 Satellite Award for Best Actor in a Series, Drama.

His many film roles include the 1987 *Long Walk to Forever* and the 2000 *The Thomas Crown Affair*, while he also provides the voice of Diego in the *Ice Age* series of animated movies.

Also on the stage, **Fletcher O'Leary**, born in 1997, is the Australian actor and dancer who since 2007 has played the character of Mickey Gannon in the long-running television soap *Neighbours*.

He was nominated for a Best Young Actor Award in Australia's 2008 Inside Soap Awards, while his younger brother, **Blake O'Leary**, is also a member of the cast of the popular soap.

Born in 1949, **Olivia O'Leary** is the award-winning current affairs presenter, journalist and author whose career began with a local newspaper in her native Republic of Ireland.

A former parliamentary sketch writer for the *Irish Times* and a current affairs presenter with the Republic's Radio Telefis Éireann (RTÉ), she later became the first regular senior female presenter of the BBC's flagship current affairs programme *Newsnight*.

During her career with RTÉ she won three Jacob's Awards for broadcasting, while in 1986 she won a Sony Award for her BBC Radio 4 programme *Between Ourselves*.

She is also the author of the 2004 book *Politicians and Other Animals*.

Also in the world of books, **Patrick O'Leary**, born in 1952 in Saginaw, Michigan, is the American fantasy and science fiction writer whose best-selling books include his 1995 *Door Number Three* and his 1998 *The Gift*, which was nominated for the World Fantasy Award.

In a different writing genre, **Brendan O'Leary** is the influential international political scientist who was born in Northern Ireland in 1958.

The author of a number of books on the Northern Ireland conflict, including, along with John McGarry, the 1999 *Policing Northern Ireland*, he has acted as a policy advisor for the British Labour Party, the European Union, the United Nations and the Kurdistan National Assembly.

At the time of writing professor of political science and director of the Penn Program in Ethnic Conflict at the University of Pennsylvania, he is also the author of the 2009 book *How to Get Out of Iraq with Integrity*.

Still in the realm of politics, **Cornelius O'Leary**, born in Limerick in 1927 and who died in 2006, was the professor of political science at Queen's University, Belfast, whose many works include his *The Northern Ireland Assembly, 1982-1986*.

Bearers of the O'Leary name have also excelled, and continue to excel, in the highly competitive world of sport.

In baseball, **Charley O'Leary** was the Major League shortstop who also provided the inspiration for two Hollywood films.

Born in Chicago in 1882, he played for the Detroit Tigers between 1904 and 1912, the St Louis Cardinals in 1913 and the St Louis Browns in 1934 – the same year he became the oldest person to appear in a game.

When not playing baseball, he and fellow player

Germany Schaefer had a successful sideline as a comic vaudeville act – an act that inspired the MGM musicals *They Learned About Women*, from 1930, and, after his death in 1941, the 1949 *Take Me Out to the Ballgame*, which starred Frank Sinatra and Gene Kelly.

Also in baseball, **Dan O'Leary**, born in Detroit in 1856 and who was nicknamed "Hustlin' Dan", was the Major League player whose teams included the Providence Grays, Detroit Wolverines and Cincinnati Outlaw Reds; he died in 1922.

On the fields of European football, **David O'Leary** is the former player who was born in 1958 in London but who moved with his family at the age of three to Dublin.

He played for English club Arsenal from 1975 to 1993, setting a club record for them of 722 appearances.

A member of the Republic of Ireland national team from 1976 to 1993, he also played for English club Leeds United in the early 1990s, and managed the club from 1998 to 2002.

Manager of Aston Villa from 2003 to 2006, he was appointed manager of Dubai Club Al-Ahli in 2010.

His brother **Pierce O'Leary**, born in 1959, is the former Irish professional footballer who, from 1979 to 1980, also played for the Republic of Ireland.

The centre-half also played for teams that include Irish team Shamrock Rovers, Canadian team the Vancouver Whitecaps and, from 1984 to 1988, Scottish Premier League club Celtic.

Keeping the sport of football in the family, his son, **Ryan O'Leary**, born in Glasgow in 1987 while his father was with Celtic, is the defender who has played for Scottish teams that include Aberdeen, Kilmarnock and Dundee.

Back to Ireland, and the Emerald Isle's popular sport of Gaelic football, **John O'Leary**, born in Dublin in 1961, is the former goalkeeper who, during his sporting career, won eight Inter-County titles with Leinster and two All-Ireland titles with the Dublin senior team – which he captained in 1986 and from 1993 to 1996.

A member of the Cork Senior Inter-County team from 2003, and a defender with his local Cill na Martra club, **Noel O'Leary** is the player who was born in 1982 in Kilnamartyra, Co. Cork.

In the equally popular Irish game of hurling, **Séanie O'Leary**, born in 1952 in Youghal, Co. Cork, is the former hurler whose local club was Youghal and who played with the Cork senior inter-county team from 1971 to 1984.

The holder of nine Munster titles and four All-Ireland titles, he is the father of the Irish rugby union player **Tómas O'Leary**.

Born in Cork in 1983, he played both Gaelic football and his father's sport of hurling before taking up rugby.

A member of the Republic of Ireland national rugby union team since 2007, he scored his first try for his country, against Italy, in the 2010 Six Nations Championship.

Back across the ocean to the United States and to a

totally different sport, **Amanda O'Leary**, born in 1967, is the top American college lacrosse coach who played for teams including Temple University and Yale University and who was enrolled into the American Lacrosse Hall of Fame in 2005.

In the ecclesiastical sphere, **Francis O'Leary**, born in 1931 in Liverpool, was the Roman Catholic priest and missionary who, in 1964, founded the international network of hospices known as Jospice.

Awarded an MBE in 1996, he died in 2000.

Born in 1879 in Richibucto, New Brunswick, **Henry O'Leary**, ordained a priest in 1901, served as the fifth Bishop of the Roman Catholic Diocese of Charlottetown before his appointment in 1920 as the third Archbishop of Edmonton.

He died in 1938, while it was his older brother, **Louis O'Leary**, born in 1877 and who died in 1930, who succeeded him in 1920 as Bishop of Charlottetown.

In the often cut-throat world of business, **Kevin O'Leary** is the Canadian entrepreneur and venture capitalist who was born in 1954 in Mount Royal, Quebec.

Setting up the computer software publisher Softkey with the aid of a $10,000 investment from his mother, he developed it into The Learning Company – selling it for a huge profit to Mattel in 1999.

He is also seen on the television screen as a venture capitalist in the Canadian version of *Dragon's Den*.

Quite literally a high-flyer in the business world, **Michael O'Leary** is the Irish businessman and airline executive who was born in 1961 in Kanturk, Co. Cork.

Graduating with a business degree in 1983, he set up a successful newsagents' business in the Republic before he was hired in 1987 as the personal financial and tax advisor to Tony Ryan, then head of Guinness Peat Aviation.

It was shortly after O'Leary's appointment that the airline Ryanair was established, and he was sent to the United States to study an American model of a 'no frills', low-cost airline.

Much of what he learned was put into effect at Ryanair, and he was appointed the airline's chief executive in 1994.

The frequently outspoken O'Leary is also a successful breeder of Aberdeen Angus cattle and racehorses – his horse *War of Attrition* winning the prestigious Cheltenham Gold Cup in 2006.

One of the most colourful and influential characters of the 'counter-culture' revolution of the 1960s and 1970s was the American psychologist and author **Dr Timothy Leary**.

Born in 1920 in Springfield, Massachusetts, he advocated the use of hallucogenic drugs such as LSD for what he perceived as their emotional and spiritual benefits, coining the phrase "Turn on, tune in, drop out."

This was a mantra taken up by the hippie generation and O'Leary as a consequence became a guru of the psychedelic experience.

Denounced by conservative elements in America, he was at one time branded "the most dangerous man in America" – a description in which he revelled – by President Richard Nixon.

Founder of the League for Spiritual Discovery, he was also author of a number of books that included his autobiographical *Flashbacks* and co-author of the best-selling *The Psychedelic Experience* – a book said to have been the inspiration for the John Lennon song *Tomorrow Never Knows*, from the Beatles *Revolver* album.

He died in May of 1996, and in a truly 'out of the world' experience of which Leary would have heartily approved, a Pegasus rocket containing seven grams of his ashes and the ashes of 24 others including *Star Trek* creator Gene Rodenberry, were fired into space.

The rocket was launched in April of 1997 and remained in celestial orbit before burning up in the atmosphere six months later.

## *Key dates in Ireland's history from the first settlers to the formation of the Irish Republic:*

| | |
|---|---|
| **circa 7000 B.C.** | Arrival and settlement of Stone Age people. |
| **circa 3000 B.C.** | Arrival of settlers of New Stone Age period. |
| **circa 600 B.C.** | First arrival of the Celts. |
| **200 A.D.** | Establishment of Hill of Tara, Co. Meath, as seat of the High Kings. |
| **circa 432 A.D.** | Christian mission of St. Patrick. |
| **800-920 A.D.** | Invasion and subsequent settlement of Vikings. |
| **1002 A.D.** | Brian Boru recognised as High King. |
| **1014** | Brian Boru killed at battle of Clontarf. |
| **1169-1170** | Cambro-Norman invasion of the island. |
| **1171** | Henry II claims Ireland for the English Crown. |
| **1366** | Statutes of Kilkenny ban marriage between native Irish and English. |
| **1529-1536** | England's Henry VIII embarks on religious Reformation. |
| **1536** | Earl of Kildare rebels against the Crown. |
| **1541** | Henry VIII declared King of Ireland. |
| **1558** | Accession to English throne of Elizabeth I. |
| **1565** | Battle of Affane. |
| **1569-1573** | First Desmond Rebellion. |
| **1579-1583** | Second Desmond Rebellion. |
| **1594-1603** | Nine Years War. |
| **1606** | Plantation' of Scottish and English settlers. |
| **1607** | Flight of the Earls. |
| **1632-1636** | Annals of the Four Masters compiled. |
| **1641** | Rebellion over policy of plantation and other grievances. |
| **1649** | Beginning of Cromwellian conquest. |
| **1688** | Flight into exile in France of Catholic Stuart monarch James II as Protestant Prince William of Orange invited to take throne of England along with his wife, Mary. |
| **1689** | William and Mary enthroned as joint monarchs; siege of Derry. |
| **1690** | Jacobite forces of James defeated by William at battle of the Boyne (July) and Dublin taken. |

| | |
|---|---|
| **1691** | Athlone taken by William; Jacobite defeats follow at Aughrim, Galway, and Limerick; conflict ends with Treaty of Limerick (October) and Irish officers allowed to leave for France. |
| **1695** | Penal laws introduced to restrict rights of Catholics; banishment of Catholic clergy. |
| **1704** | Laws introduced constricting rights of Catholics in landholding and public office. |
| **1728** | Franchise removed from Catholics. |
| **1791** | Foundation of United Irishmen republican movement. |
| **1796** | French invasion force lands in Bantry Bay. |
| **1798** | Defeat of Rising in Wexford and death of United Irishmen leaders Wolfe Tone and Lord Edward Fitzgerald. |
| **1800** | Act of Union between England and Ireland. |
| **1803** | Dublin Rising under Robert Emmet. |
| **1829** | Catholics allowed to sit in Parliament. |
| **1845-1849** | The Great Hunger: thousands starve to death as potato crop fails and thousands more emigrate. |
| **1856** | Phoenix Society founded. |
| **1858** | Irish Republican Brotherhood established. |
| **1873** | Foundation of Home Rule League. |
| **1893** | Foundation of Gaelic League. |
| **1904** | Foundation of Irish Reform Association. |
| **1913** | Dublin strikes and lockout. |
| **1916** | Easter Rising in Dublin and proclamation of an Irish Republic. |
| **1917** | Irish Parliament formed after Sinn Fein election victory. |
| **1919-1921** | War between Irish Republican Army and British Army. |
| **1922** | Irish Free State founded, while six northern counties remain part of United Kingdom as Northern Ireland, or Ulster; civil war up until 1923 between rival republican groups. |
| **1949** | Foundation of Irish Republic after all remaining constitutional links with Britain are severed. |